Anonymous

A Brief Sketch of Shelby

A thriving town in the Piedmont section of North Carolina

Anonymous

A Brief Sketch of Shelby

A thriving town in the Piedmont section of North Carolina

ISBN/EAN: 9783337254384

Printed in Europe, USA, Canada, Australia, Japan

Cover: Foto ©ninafisch / pixelio.de

More available books at **www.hansebooks.com**

A BRIEF SKETCH

—OF—

SHELBY,

A Thriving Town

IN THE

PIEDMONT SECTION

Of North Carolina.

SHELBY, N. C.
C. P. Roberts, Book and Job Printer,
1889.

The sender of this pamphlet calls your attention to page 2

INTRODUCTION.

In presenting this little book to the public, it is designed to give them facts only, believing, as we do, that if the public generally knew of our superb climate and other advantages, that many would be impelled to come and settle among us and help further develop our town and County. With this object in view, we send it forth and invite all to visit us and be convinced. Shelby is destined to be a Railroad centre, a summer resort, and a town of commercial importance.

Shelby is full of pluck, energy and enterprise. Only last fall one of her finest brick blocks was burned to the ground; to-day it is all rebuilt, substantial, in modern style, and an ornament to any town. No capital remains idle around Shelby; it pays to invest it and all do invest and receive handsome profits. Every day new advantages open up and more money can be used to advantage. The whole town invites capital and population of pushing and go ahead people, no idlers are wanted. A large Hotel in modern style would be a paying investment now. A street car line to Cleveland Springs (distant two miles) would pay. It will pay to invest in Real Estate now. Cotton Factories pay. We could go on and mention many things that would pay, but space forbids. Read the different articles in this pamphlet and see what has been done and what is doing.

Any information in regard to anything about Shelby will be cheerfully answered by the Clerk of the Town Council, or C. E. FRICK, Real Estate Agent.

—A—

BRIEF SKETCH OF

SHELBY,

A Thriving Town in

The Piedmont Section

—OF—

NORTH CAROLINA.

Shelby, the county seat of Cleveland County, derived its name from Colonel Shelby, an American officer in the Revolutionary war, and a hero of the great and important battle fought at King's Mountain, this county.

The town is beautifully located near the geographical centre of the County. The streets are broad, and laid off with regularity.

The central square of the town is the property of the county, and is a remarkably pretty green, or small park, containing many handsome elms, maples, and trees of other varieties. The County Court House, containing the court room and the offices of the county officials, stands in this square. An engraving of the Court Square constitutes the frontispiece of this pamphlet.

A magnificent view of the Blue Ridge Mountain is obtained from Shelby. The town is nestled among the foot hills of that mountain range. The natural drainage is excellent, the climate healthful and invigorating, and the site picturesque and charming. The altitude of the town is about one thousand feet above the sea level. It is one of the most beautiful small towns in the United States, its population having increased from 900, in 1880, to 2,500 in 1889. Within the town limits are mineral springs possessing valuable medicinal properties, and within two miles of the Court House are the world-famed Cleveland White Sulphur and Chalybeate Springs; also within four miles are Patterson's Springs, noted far and wide for their healing properties, more fully described elsewhere in these pages. The seasons are mild and salubrious. During the past winter (1888-'89) we had but one snow storm, and within twelve hours every vestige of the snow had entirely disappeared. The summer's heat is tempered by gentle mountain breezes; the sweltering, oppressive, dog-day weather so well known elsewhere, and often experienced even in New York and the Eastern states, is here unknown, and bed-clothing can not be dispensed with, even in the midst of the hot season.

We have two trunk lines of Railroad which connect us with the outside world, viz: the Carolina Central, whose seaport terminus is Wilmington, N. C., and the Charleston, Cincinnati & Chicago Railroad. These roads intersect and connect with the great railways systems of the South and carry four daily mails. The main line of the Richmond & Danville Railroad also passes through the county, South of Shelby, the Charleston, Cincinnati & Chicago Railroad connecting with and crossing it at Blacksburg, S. C., about twelve miles south-west of Shelby, making close connection both North and South. The Carolina Central being a part of the great Seaboard Air-Line, makes close connection at Wadesboro with the Atlantic Coast Line for all points South, and at Hamlet with Raleigh & Augusta Air-Line for Norfolk, Washington, Baltimore and all points North, Work is rapidly progressing on the division of the South-Western Air-Line Railroad from Shelby to

Morganton, about twenty-five miles being already graded, steel rails contracted for, and in a few months we will have connection with the Richmond & Danville system at Morganton for Asheville, N. C., Knoxville, Tenn., etc.

Shelby has more than doubled its population in the past five years. Its houses are all new and built in modern styles.

TOWN COUNCIL:

Mayor—W. L. Damron.

Aldermen—S. G. Brice, M. L. Carroll, G. L. Leak and C. V. Bostic.

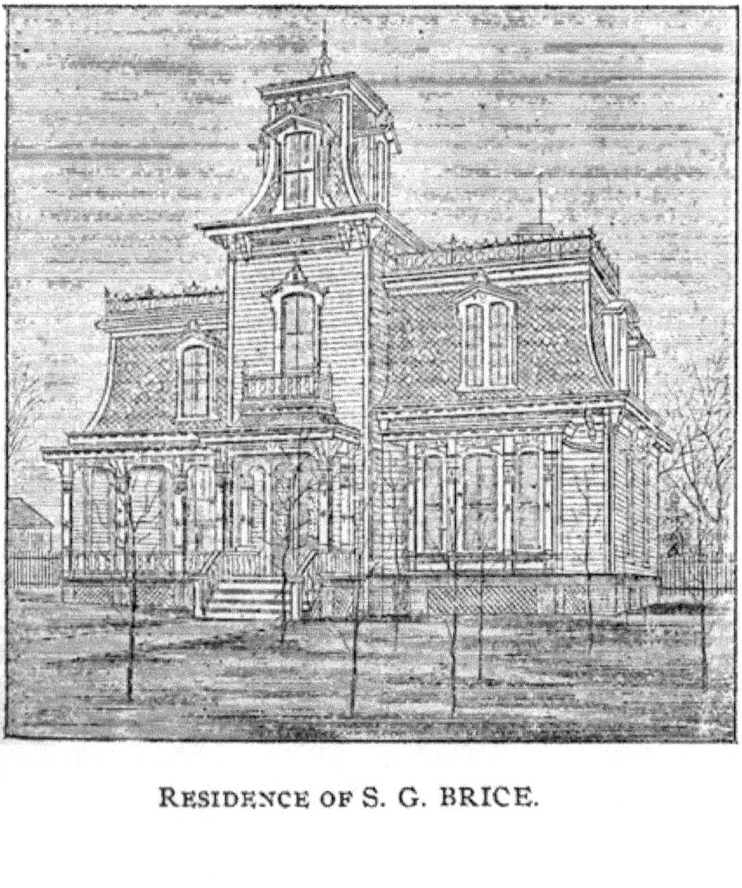

RESIDENCE OF S. G. BRICE.

CLEVELAND COUNTY.

Population 20,000; 420 square miles. Cleveland is comparatively a new county. It was formed in 1841 from the counties of Rutherford and Lincoln. It is bounded on the South by the State of South Carolina; joins Gaston, Burke, Rutherford and Lincoln counties; contains 275,000 acres of fertile land; has 2500 farms, about 90,000 acres of improved land. No fences, except around county and pastures. This county belongs to the Piedmont belt of the State. The soil is principally clay. Every thing that grows in North Carolina can be grown in Cleveland County with more or less profit.

It is watered by the two Broad Rivers and several large creeks, along which are thousands of acres of the richest alluvial bottoms to be found in any of the old coast States. One of these creeks—Buffalo—is particularly noted for the large quantity and fertility of its bottoms. This remarkable stream has its source at the foot of South Mountain, in the extreme North, and flows the entire length of the county. For twenty miles it will average a hundred acres of low lands to the mile. These low lands are especially adapted to the growth of corn, and the yield is enormous. Corn also does well on the uplands, as much as 75 bushels per acre having been raised. That amount is above the average for uplands.

Cotton does well, the average per acre being about 900 pounds of seed cotton, but it is said this soil is capable of producing 2500 pounds per acre very easily. The weed does not grow large, but fruits well.

Wheat is one of the best paying products. The product of the county reaches perhaps 300,000 bushels, and very little attention is paid to its culture.

Oats do well, and our people are beginning to pay more attention to their culture, 60 bushels per acre being made on uplands with very little fertilizers.

Sweet potatoes do well, the supply being so plentiful that during harvesting time they can be bought at from 20 to 30 cents per bushel, and even now—April 1st—the supply is plentiful at 50 cents per bushel.

Irish Potatoes yield largely, and the supply is usually abundant, the price ranging at from 50 to 75 cents per bushel.

Clover and grasses grow to perfection, and much interest is being manifested in their culture.

RESIDENCE OF MAJ. H. D. LEE.

Our land is well adapted to the growth of Tobacco, but our people in this county do not take to its culture.

Sorghum cane is grown here with a great deal of profit, about eighty to one hundred gallons being made to the acre, and selling at from 30 to 50 cents per gallon. The seed is used for stock feed and is worth about $5 per acre; even the blades are utilized and furnish feed for stock. This sorghum molasses has very much lessened the sale of New Orleans and other like goods in this section in the last few years.

Fruits and vegetables all do well. Dr. L. N. Durham has tried truck farming on a small scale for the past few years, and finds it pays so well that he will soon convert all his plantation into Orchards, Vineyards, Strawberries, Vegetables, Clover and Grasses. He has all the best and earliest varieties of Peaches, Strawberries and Grapes, which pay him handsomely for his efforts.

There are several small vineyards in Shelby that pay their owners handsome profits. The largest of these has about 15 acres in all the earliest and best varieties. From it is sold a great quantity to the Shelby people, but still more are made into the finest wines to be found, always bringing a good price, with a market not far away.

Dried fruits—such as Peaches, Apples, Blackberries, Plums, etc., are invariably shipped from this place to the Northern markets in large quantities, paying the shipper.

The timbers in this County are of many kinds, and in great abundance. Shelby would be a good point for a Spoke and Handle Factory. The timber is close and abundant and the shipping facilities good. See letter from Mr. L. E. Powers on the Forests.

COUNTY OFFICERS:

T. D. LATTIMORE, Clerk Superior Court.
M. N. HAMRICK, Sheriff.
J. F. WILLIAMS, Register of Deeds
J. S. WRAY, Treasurer.

COTTON MILLS.

The Belmont Cotton Mills are located upon the line of the Charleston, Cincinnati & Chicago Railroad, three-quarters of a mile south of the court house, in Shelby. Though a new enterprise (having been put in operation in 1887,) it has produced from the outset handsome returns for the owners, Messrs. Miller, Blanton & Oates. The actual capital invested is about $65,000. The machinery is new and of the most recent designs. About 3,100 spindles are kept busily whirling both day and night. The monthly pay roll makes glad the hearts of one hundred and twenty operatives, and adds not a little to the prosperity of the town. The factory buildings are substantially constructed of brick, and are not wanting in architectural beauty. The rooms are lighted by electricity. Steam is the motive power, and is produced from cord-wood fuel. The cord-wood delivered at the factory is worth $1.25 per cord. The product of the mill is in demand, and orders for the output for some time to come are on file in the office.

On the opposite side of town from the Belmont Mills, and about the same distance from the centre, are the Shelby Cotton Mills, owned and operated by Messrs. Morgan, Cline & Co. This mill is of brick, and has been built since the Belmont. It is a model factory of its dimensions. The cash investment is $25,000. Their machinery is run on full time to meet the large demand for the product, which is carpet warp. An eighty horse-power Corliss engine turns their 2,500 spindles. Both the Belmont and Shelby Mills are owned by local business men, not one dollar of outside capital having been solicited or used.

Within the County, and near Shelby, are several fine cotton factories. The Laurel Mills, 3½ miles from Shelby on Broad River, are the property of Maj. R. B. Miller, a prominent business man of the town. The new buildings have recently been completed and about 2,000 spindles are already in operation. The sum of $30,000 has up to this time been invested, while important improvements are steadily being made. The water-power of the river is here utilized.

A few miles north of town upon Broad River, are the Cleveland Cotton Mills, the largest in the County. A substantial new brick building of two stories has recently been completed, and 5,100 spindles are now in operation. These mills are the property of an incorporated Company, and are superintended by Maj. H. F Sceuck, a large holder of the stock. Mr. Reynolds, a prominent commission merchant of New York City, is interested to a considerable extent in the enterprise. Many car loads of machinery have lately been placed in position.

At King's Mountain, in the south-eastern part of the county, on the line of the Richmond & Danville Railroad, a new cotton factory will soon be in operation. A new brick building has been erected and the machinery is now on hand and is being placed in position. The capital was subscribed upon the co-operative plan.

Several new cotton factories are proposed, and will doubtless ere long become realities; but as we desire to limit the information conveyed by this little book to substantial and existing facts, we forbear to describe any such schemes which may have connected with them an element of uncertainty.

WATER-POWERS.

Many fine water-powers are found upon the streams in this county. Stice's Shoals, on Broad River, near the C., C. & C. R. R., are owned by Dr. R. H. Morrison, of Shelby. The entire volume of water in the river can be utilized, the fall being 14 feet or more. Dr. Morrison estimates that 3,000 horse-power is here available.

Mr. W. J. Roberts has a fine water-power on Buffalo creek, where the fall is at least 17 feet. This power is upon a fine tract of farming land containing 415 acres, many acres being rich bottoms. See Mr. Roberts' advertisement further on in this book.

FOUNDRY AND MACHINE SHOPS.

The Shelby Foundry and Machine Shops are superintended by Mr. B. B. Babington. Mr. Babington is a natural mechanic, and has had the advantage of a life-long training at his business in Pennsylvania, Tennessee, Alabama, and at this place. He is a thoroughly practical and experienced foundry-man and machinist, having been connected with these trades from boyhood. Mr. Babington is a native of Pittsburgh, Pa., the great centre of the iron and steel industries of this country. He purchased this old established business in 1875, and has carried it on with ever increasing success. These works turn out machinery of various kinds, such as Cane Mills, Mining Stamp Mills, Evaporators, Plows, Stove Castings, &c., and a general machine and repair business is done. He has every facility for making castings weighing from one ounce to a ton.

——o——

SASH, BLIND AND DOOR FACTORIES.

Mr. L. E. Powers has a factory well furnished with wood-working machinery. He turns out Sash, Blinds, Doors, Brackets, Fencing, &c., runs Planing Machines, and does a general wood-working business. Mr. Powers is an active, intelligent business man. He has several times represented Cleveland County in the General Assembly of this State. He is an authority in matters concerning the lumber trade. A short article on the lumber interests of Cleveland County by him will be found on another page.

M. E. Rudasill, Contractor and Builder, also operates a Sash, Blind and Door Factory.

——o——

WAGON AND BUGGY SHOPS.

J. W. Lineberger & Son are an old and well-established house. They manufacture Wagons and Buggies, noted for their strength, beauty and durability. This firm has recently fitted up a new brick building on Warren street, and in these commodious quarters have every facility for doing fine work in their line. They are prepared to do blacksmithing and wheelwright work of all kinds. Both father and son give personal attention to the business.

———

Mr. A. W. Eskridge has recently purchased the old Shelby Foundry and Machine Shop buildings and will remodel the buildings and enlarge his Wagon and Buggy Manufactory. Mr. Eskridge makes neat and desirable vehicles of all kinds. He is well equipped for repairing on short notice, and does all kinds of wood and blacksmith work in first-class style. Mr. Eskridge is a native of Cleveland county, and does a large business.

FORESTS.

Perhaps no section of the United States produces a greater variety of timber than the Piedmont section of North Carolina. There are sections in which the trees grow much larger—as, for instance, the trees of California and the "Poplar" of Tennessee; but where these large trees are found, they have a kind of monopoly of the soil and not much else of value is found. In Piedmont North Carolina, and particularly in Cleveland county, which occupies the most favorable position in all that belt, nearly every species of timber, indigenous to this climate, is found in sufficient quantity and of sufficient size to meet the wants of a very extended development of the mechanic arts. Nearly every species of oak may be found here—White, Red, Black Spanish, Post and Chestnut Oak, each having its peculiar fitness for certain purposes in the various industries. The Chestnut Oak is found on elevated ridges and foot hills of mountains and on the mountains. All other species are found in profusion all over the county. Perhaps the most valuable timber, and that found in the greatest quantity, is the Pine. It has been more generally utilized for building and manufacturing purposes than other timbers. The others are simply awaiting the introduction and development of such industries as will utilize them. There are several species of the White Leaf Pine, the natural growth of this county, differing only in texture, but not in utility. This Pine is a splendid building

material, and quite an extensive lumbering business is being done. Old and abandoned fields are soon reforested with a growth of pine called Old Field Pine. The growth of this Pine is rapid, forming a forest in fifteen or twenty years of suitable size for fence rails and fuel, for which it is most admirably adapted, and restoring the exhausted soil to its original virgin fertility. Poplar large enough for mechanical purposes may be found everywhere. The forests, however, grow on the mountain sides in the upper portion of the county. In that same upper portion on the mountains, there is an immense forest of White Pine of enormous size, but so remote from mills and market that it has never been utilized, but will some day form a source of wealth to its mountain owners. Hickory of splendid quality may be found everywhere; the only use, however, to which it has been put, is for fuel and to supply the little home demand for axletrees, &c. Persimmon and dog-wood grow spontaneously, and ought to be valuable for shuttle blocks, and such other things as they are adapted to make. Maple may be found along all the water courses and on wet lands. Walnut is tolerably abundant in some portions of the county. This county was once well stocked with chestnut, but from cause, supposed to be severe drouths, the trees have nearly all died, and their dry gourd forms may be found standing or lying in all woods. Beach, Birch, Ash, Sycamore and other timbers may be found in limited quantities.

L. E. POWERS.

———o———

PROFESSIONS.

The professions are all well filled in Shelby by intelligent and accomplished gentlemen. The names of some of the representative members of each profession will be here mentioned:

Dr. L. N. Durham, Surgeon Dentist, is a veteran in his calling, having been practicing for thirty-five years. He has more than a local reputation. Dr. Durham can be depended upon for fine work in his line.

———

Dr. J. A. Harrill is a Surgeon Dentist of known ability. He is an expert in his profession, and needs no recommendation with the people of Cleveland county.

Gidney & Webb, Attorneys and Counselors at Law, are an old established firm. Capt. J. W. Gidney is the senior member of the firm. Mr. J. L. Webb, the junior member of the firm, is well and favorably known throughout the State. He has twice represented Cleveland and Gaston counties in the State Senate.

Wood & Schenck, Attorneys and Counsellors at Law, practice in the State and Federal Courts, and give prompt and careful attention to all business put in their hands. One of the firm (Mr. Wood) is a Commissioner for the State of South Carolina.

McBrayer & Ryburn, Attorneys at Law, are an old established firm. They practice in all the courts, and are the agents in this county of the British and American Loan Association. Their office is located on Marion St., opposite the Court House.

J A. Anthony has lately entered at the bar and opened a law office in Shelby. He is the County Superintendent of Public Instruction, and is well known in this locality. He solicits business in his line.

———O———

MINERALS

And Mineral Waters of Cleveland Co.

North Carolina has been aptly termed "the Mineralogist's Paradise." It is a fact that a greater variety of minerals occur within its bounds than are to be found in any other state of the Union, and of these minerals a very large proportion exist in the county of Cleveland. A few of the more important will be mentioned in this short article. The presence of large beds of pyrites and other minerals, through which water percolates, taking up in solution many of the curative and health-giving mineral elements, accounts for the famous mineral springs, so many of which exist in this famed region. Some of the most renowned of these springs are in Cleveland, and a few of them will be mentioned further on.

First of the minerals,

GOLD.

Gold is distributed through the entire county. It is everywhere disseminated to some extent throughout the soil, and exists in the sands of the various streams. The beds of creeks and of spring branches have been worked in many localities with more or less success, very primitive apparatus having in such cases been used. The largest yields, however, have been received from the vein mines, of which there are several. The King's Mountain gold mine has been worked to a depth approximating 400 feet, the vein is of immense size, in places forty feet wide. The vein being in limestone, and carrying a very small percentage of sulphurets, can be easily worked and the ores economically milled, so that material of very low grade is profitably handled. A product of $750,000 is credited to this mine. The McEntyre mine within a few miles of Shelby has produced some good ore, but is not now being worked.

SILVER

occurs only sparingly in small veins of agentiferous galena.

IRON.

Iron, in a number of its different ores, is abundant in the county, and of very fine quality. About King's Mountain are banks and veins of magnetite and hematite which have been worked to a considerable extent. Many of the veins carry ores which are to a high degree manganiferous, and valuable in the manufacture of spiegeleisen. Lime is close at hand for fluxing, there being a very heavy vein extending for miles in a northeasterly and southwesterly direction, parallel with the iron veins.

TIN.

Cassiterite, the most valuable ore of tin, has recently been found to extend over a considerable area about the town of King's Mountain. The ore is of high grade, carrying a very large percentage of metallic tin. The quantity of ore which may be made available has not yet been determined, but promises to be large. The exploration of these deposits has been undertaken by capitalists of large experience in mining, and important developments are expected.

VIEW ON SUMTER STREET.

MICA.

Statistics show that about 60 per cent. of the Mica, used in the United States, is produced in North Carolina: and it is a fact in the history of mining in the State that the first good and merchantable mica produced since the days of the pre-historic mound-builders, was mined in Cleveland County in the year 1867, and marketed in New York by Hon. T. L. Clingman. Other counties, notably—Mitchell and Yancey—now take the front rank as to the quantity of the yield, but in quality the Cleveland mica is unsurpassed. The census of 1880 shows that the annual product of the mica mines was ten times the entire amount of the capital employed. The preparation of the mica for market is entirely by hand work, and the process exceedingly simple; the blocks, as they come from the mine, after passing through the hands of a "dresser," who strikes off the foreign material or gauge, are split into thin layers and go to the "scuber," who is supplied with a number of tin or sheet iron patterns of the different sizes demanded by the trade; he lays the patterns on the mica and rapidly marks the sheet with a knife or sharp-pointed instrument; the "cutter" then with shears cuts out the pieces, following the lines made by the marker. The mineral is then packed, boxed and shipped.

SOME OTHER MINERALS.

Copper is found in the form of chalcopyrite, and other of its ores. A nugget of native copper, weighing perhaps an ounce, was found by a farmer in digging a ditch on his land. He brought it to the writer for examination, evidently supposing that he had a lump of gold. This is the only instance of the finding of native copper which has come to my attention.

Corundum is found in scattered specimens.

Pyclonsite, and other ores of manganese, exist in quantities which may perhaps pay for working. Some specimens sent by me to Pittsburg for analysis gave good returns.

Koolin and fire-clay are found.

Several veins of Graphite are known in the county. Some very handsome specimens have been taken from them, but it is believed that no work of importance has been done.

Soapstone is common, and is used for hearths, grave-stones, &c.

Granite, syenyte, gneiss and other building stones occur in great quantity in various parts of the county.

Diamonds have been found in the surrounding counties, fine specimens having come from Rutherford on the west, and Lincoln on the east, and without doubt these exist in the gravel-beds of this county. The itacolumyte, which by many experts is considered the true matrix of the diamond, is here.

Beryl is common, and some handsome aqua-marines have been found.

Garnet is widely distributed, occurring in many of our rocks.

Quartz Crystals of great beauty are of common occurrence, among which are cairingorm or smokey-quartz, rose-quartz, crystals enclosing sand, globules of water, &c.

MINERAL WATERS.

Two miles from Shelby are the world-famed Cleveland Springs. There are here springs of white sulphur, red sulphur and chalybeate waters. The white sulphur water is thought by many physicians and experts to be superior to the white sulphur springs of Virginia. These waters have many times been analysed with results as follows:

WHITE SULPHUR SPRINGS.

One Gallon of Water Contains:

4.80 inches	Sulphuretted Hydrogen gas and Carbonic Acid.
4.50 Grains	Carbonate of Lime.
18.70 Grains	Sulphate of Lime.
4.80 Grains	Muriate of Lime.
7.65 Grains	Muriate of Magnesia.

IODINE, OR RED SULPHUR SPRING.

One Gallon of Water contains:

4.22 Cubic inches	Sulphuretted Hydrogen Gas and Carbonic Acid.
3.12 Grains	Carbonate of Lime.
17.32 Grains	Sulphate Lime, Iodine and Magnesia.

CHALYBEATE SPRING.

One Gallon of Water contains:

12.50 Grains	Carbonate of Protoxide of Iron
1.50 Grs.	Carbonate Lime; traces of Sulphate Lime and Magnesia

This property is in the hands of intelligent and progressive managers, and ample arrangements exist for the entertainment and pleasure of guests.

Patterson's Springs, about four miles south-east of Shelby, are similar in character to the Cleveland Springs. There also are the white and red sulphur and chalybeate waters. A summer boarding house is kept by Mr. Patterson. These springs are near Patterson's station, on the C., C. & C. R. R.

Within the incorporate limits of Shelby, and but a few minutes' walk from the court house, are the Hoke chalybeate springs. These waters are strongly impregnated with iron, and their medicinal qualities are held in high esteem in the locality.

Many other mineral springs exist in both town and county which to describe, would be merely to reproduce and repeat what has already been said of those above mentioned, and it will suffice to say here that nature has richly and plentifully endowed us with mineral waters possessing prophylactic and healing properties, such as are rarely found and nowhere excelled. B. F. W.

———O———

SHELBY, N. C.,

One of the Most Progressive Towns in the State.

Is as healthful a place as is to be found in Western North Carolina. Always fanned by the mountain breeze; has pure air and good water; population 2500; the popuation has doubled in five years. 1000 feet above sea level.

Two cotton factories, giving employment to 200 hands.

Seven wood and iron shops.

Two extensive wagon and buggy manufactories.

Two iron machine and foundry shops.

Two sash and blind factories.

One banking house.

Thirty dry goods and grocery houses.

Two furniture establishments. Three drug stores.

One Military Institute, with new $8,000 building.

One female college in a flourishing condition.

Several private schools with good patronage.

Five white and three colored churches.

Two railroads and another one building.

Three telegraphic lines.

Two splendid livery and feed stables.

One music house—organs, small instruments, sheet music, &c.

Three millinery establishments.

One fifteen-acre vineyard and a dozen small ones.

One poultry yard, and one marble yard.

A presidential post-office, with $1600 salary.

The streets are lighted by gasoline.

RESIDENCE OF S. J. GREEN.

Two harness shops. One marble yard.

Three large hotels. Guests always leave satisfied.

Several boarding houses in and out of town.

Three-acre court square, a beautiful park, with nice bench seats and lovely shades.

Broad, shady streets and many handsome dwellings.

One Masonic Lodge. Two nice barber shops.

One Y. M. C. A. hall. One bakery. One opera hall.

Two good newspapers and three job printing offices

Three tin and copper shops.

A first-class Potographic Gallery.

One excellent iron and several freestone springs inside of town. Within a few minutes' drive are the noted Cleveland and Patterson Sulphur Springs.

From Shelby to Charlotte, via C. C. Railroad, only 54 miles.

TABLE of DISTANCES from SHELBY —TO—

	Miles.		Miles.
Cleveland Springs	2	Gaffney City, S. C.	20
Patterson's Springs	4	Lincolnton	22
Double Shoals	8	Logan's Store	24
Beam's Mills	8	Rutherfordton	25
Grover	10	Dallas	25
Mooresboro	10	Brittain	30
King's Mountain	14	Spartanburg, S. C	37
Cherryville	11	Morganton	40
Black's	14	Marion	40
Cleveland Mills	13	Chimney Rock	42
Belwood	16	Hendersonville	55
Forest City	19	Asheville	65

OUR CHURCHES, ETC.

METHODIST.

The Methodists have an elegant brick church on Marion street, opposite the court square. Preaching is held every Sabbath morning and evening. Rev. J. T. Finlayson, Pastor.

THE EPISCOPALIANS

have an ancient looking but comfortable church, situated on LaFayette street. Services one Sabbath in each month, morning and evening. Rev. A. N. Nixon, Rector.

THE BAPTISTS

have a very good frame building, situated on LaFayette street, but are preparing to build this summer a handsome brick church to cost $6,000. The contract to build the new church has been let, and part of the material is now on the ground. Preaching every Sabbath morning and evening. Rev. J. M. McManaway. Pastor.

THE PRESBYTERIANS

have a neat frame church on corner of Graham and DeKalb streets. They also own a neat parsonage on Washington street. Services are held two Sabbaths in each month, morning and evening. Rev. ———— ————, Pastor.

BELMONT CHAPEL,

for use of the operatives of Belmont Cotton Mills, is a neat little wooden structure on south Washington street. Sunday-school every Sabbath evening and preaching occasionally.

THE Y. M. C. A.

occupy the entire second floor of J. H. Hightower's building on Marion street, first door east of where Bostic Bros. & Wright's building stood. In this building the society has three elegant rooms. Though yet in its infancy much good has already been done. The furniture and library are not yet complete, but there is money enough on hand and subscribed to complete them. The Association meets every Tuesday night and Sunday afternoon.

MASONIC LODGE.

Shelby boasts of one of the brightest and best Lodges in the State. It was organized December 7th, 1858; has 85 members and owns a nice brick hall 30x100 feet. The Lodge meets regularly once a month.

————O————

OUR SCHOOLS.

SHELBY MILITARY INSTITUTE.

The Shelby Military Institute was opened September 12th, 1887, under the joint management of its present principals, Capt. W. T. R. Bell and S. E. Gidney. Prof. Gidney was already most favorably known to the people of Shelby as a teacher. Capt. Bell was the founder of the King's Mountain High School and its Principal for eleven years. During its first year the Shelby Military

Institute has been liberally patronized at home and largely from abroad, its register showing such numbers as few of the strictly male schools in the State unconnected with the public school system, have reached. Arrangements are now made to enlarge its advantages by giving ample buildings. Buildings and grounds costing eight thousand dollars will be ready for occupacy by October 1st, 1889. It is easy to see that Shelby will soon have a school attracting the attention, not only of Western North and South Carolina, but of many of the Southern States.

The object of the School is, by a thorough course, to prepare students for College and the University, or young men for the business pursuits of life.

Students in the Classical Course, preparing for College, are allowed to follow the order of text-books named in the course of the Institution for which they are preparing.

In the Select or Business Course, students are drilled in those studies which have a special relation to commercial life.

This School is thoroughly academic, and does not arrogate to itself claims to which it is not entitled. It does not propose to advertise as a College and then fall below the results and advantages that might be reasonably expected of a well-conducted primary school. While offering a thorough classical and mathematical course—taking up in its order the junior and senior studies of our colleges, it is thoroughly academic in its drill—seeking to train the mind by healthful development, into analytical methods, and requiring at every step blackboard illustrations. It scope is well defined in rising between the primary neighborhood school on the one hand, and the lecture system of the college on the other. Distinct from each, yet partaking of the advantages of both, it forms a connecting link between the two. The need of such institutions must be felt in States which have not yet fully established, as they should do, proper systems of graded schools.

The Military feature of this School is adopted purely as a matter of discipline, and to afford systematic and healthful exercise for the students. The corps is drilled after school hours, and the drill will in no way interfere with the course of studies. All boys over fourteen years of age are required to join the corps, unless especially excused. The arm used is the U. S. Cadet Rifle—a light and beautiful piece.

SHELBY FEMALE COLLEGE.

This is a handsome three-story brick building, at a cost of about $12,000, and would be an ornament to any city. It is located on Washington street, one of the prettiest streets in town, and is convenient to all the churches. The building has three piazzas, each about 200 feet long, for exercise during inclement weather.

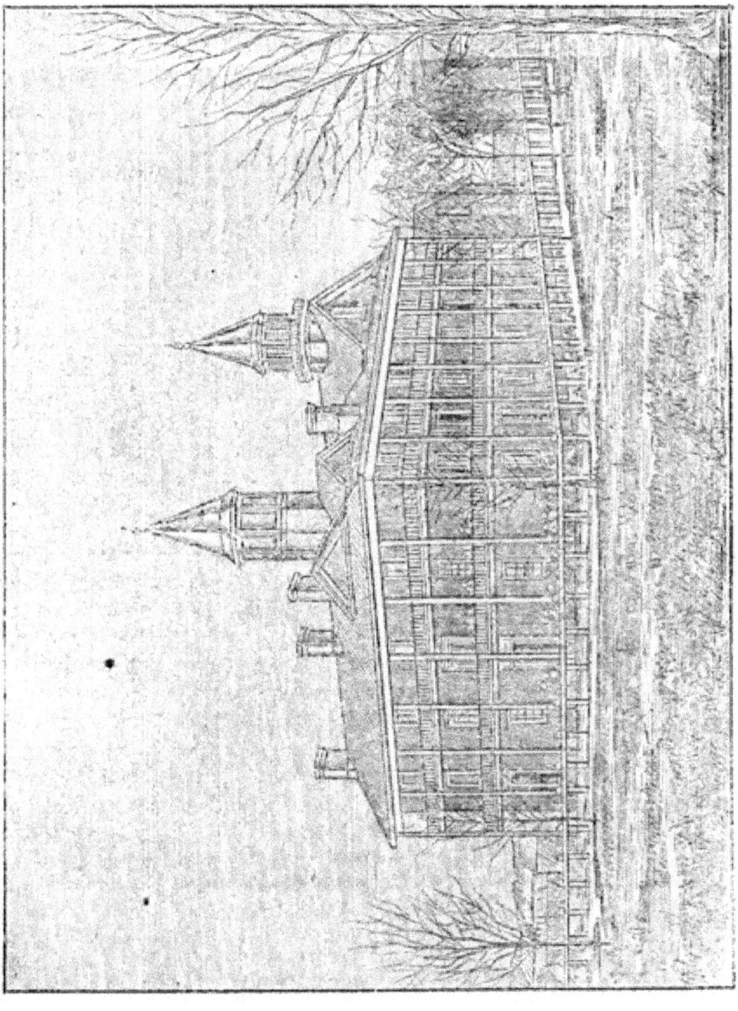

SHELBY FEMALE COLLEGE.

The rooms are large, airy, and well furnished. From the observatory of this building can be had a magnificent view of the Blue Ridge, King's Mountain, and a full view of the whole town of Shelby.

This institution was incorporated under the laws of North Carolina, February 22d, 1883, and has had a good patronage ever since its organization. Mrs. J. A. McDonald, the present principal, needs no recommendation to the people of North Carolina, and we may confidently expect to see this school continue to prosper and grow under her supervision. See advertisement on another page in this book.

RESIDENCE OF HON. R. MCBRAYER.

SHELBY NEEDS—

More cotton factories,
A first-class hotel building,
Several furniture factories,
Shuttle block factories,
Some shoe factories,
Good flouring mills,
Some wholesale mercantile houses,
Progressive and thrifty new-comers,
Any enterprise that will utilize our raw materials,
Most of all else more cash capital.

L. H. HARRILL & CO.

We all hope not to need the services of this firm very soon. In fact, the town of Shelby is so very healthful that their home patronage (although they get it all) is not very great. They do fine work at reasonable prices, and ship a great deal to other points. Any one needing work in their line will do well to call on them. See advertisement elsewhere.

MILLER BROS.

This firm is composed of A. C. and Maj. R. B. Miller, and is one of the oldest and most substantial firms in Shelby. They carry a full line of general merchandise, and are large cotton buyers. Both of these gentlemen are large real estate owners in and around Shelby.

THE NEW ERA.

The "New Era," published by Geo. A. and C. E. Frick, is a first-class weekly newspaper, always fresh, newsy and spicy, giving the latest news up to hour of going to press. The New Era is said, by competent judges, to be one of the best papers published in the Piedmont section of North Carolina A new power press is used, its type is good, and presents a neat appearance.

J. A. WRAY

has one of the best equipped livery stables in Western North Carolina. His horses are good, vehicles first-class, and drivers polite and attentive. Mr. Wray prides himself upon keeping gentle horses for his customers, and finds it a good business principle to follow this rule. His vehicles meet all trains to convey passengers anywhere they wish to go. Parties desiring special turnouts can be accommodated by writing or telegraphing ahead.

THE CENTRAL HOTEL

is a large three-story brick building fronting court square. The rooms are large and airy, and a grand view of the Blue Ridge mountains can be had from the observatory of this building. Mr. W. E. Ryburn, the proprietor, is a genial and capable host, and is now making special preparation for the summer visitors.

MARTIN & WARE.

This firm carries a full line of plain and fancy groceries, confectioneries, &c They make a specialty of flour, and, as they are agents for good flouring mills, they can easily compete in prices. Their sales are tremendous for a town of this size.

M'BRAYER & WILSON.

Dr. V. McBrayer, of this firm, is a graduate of the Medical University, city of New York. He has been very successful in the practice of medicine, and is daily becoming more popular. He is in copartnership with Mr. H. D. Wilson in the drug business, and they keep a first-class store. They have a spacious room 100 feet long, handsomely fitted up. They purchased new, last year, an elegant Arctic soda fountain at a cost of $1,500, and constantly keep all the latest cool drinks.

MALLARD & LEAK.

Necessary to every town is a first-class meat market. In this, Shelby is second to none, as Messrs. Mallard & Leak furnish fresh, every day, the choicest of meats and at moderate prices.

WATT ELLIOTT,

the ever clever, kind and obliging Shelby barber, is noted for all the above qualities, and more,—he always gives a good shave, is always in a good humor and a general favorite with everybody that knows him. Of Watt too much cannot be said. He always employs experienced assistants.

J. P. NELSON

runs two establishments here,—one on LaFayette street, the other on Railroad street, near C. C. depot. He deals in family groceries, confectioneries, fruits, &c., &c. Mr. Nelson is a practical printer, but prefers merchandising, and sells a great many goods.

D. D. SUTTLE,

ex-sheriff of Cleveland county, and a progressive man, has done a great deal for the building up of Shelby. He is a large real estate owner in and around town. One of the most important enterprises of Shelby he has started in the last six months—that of a water-power grist mill to furnish daily, for the public, fresh corn meal; also of preparing stock feed ready for use. This is done by means of a corn and cob crusher, which adds much to the value of the stock feed, and at a little cost. His mill and premises are picturesque and full of ingenuity. He has pipes from his pond, which convey water to all his stock; also from his spring to the milk house, with many kindred improvements. A visit to his premises will pay any one. Mr. Suttle has some valuable real estate for sale, and any one wishing to buy will do well to call on him.

CAROLINA CENTRAL RAILROAD.

This road runs from Wilmington, N. C., to Rutherfordton, N. C., and is one of the safest roads in the world. You rarely hear of an accident on it, and its trains are always on time. The coaches are splendid and the conductors polite and obliging. This road runs daily mail and passenger trains; makes close connection at Charlotte for all points North and South; connects at Wadesboro for Florence, S. C, etc.; at Hamlet for Raleigh, etc.; at Maxton for Bennettsville, S. C., Fayetteville. N. C., etc. This road has abandoned the wooden trestles, and instead have built all iron bridges. The iron bridge across First Broad River, near Shelby, is a perfect beauty. About one hundred miles of this road is perfectly straight, with not a perceptible crook in it. Train leaves Shelby at 9.22 a. m., arriving at Charlotte at 12.05 p. m.; returning, leave Charlotte at 4.15 p. m., arriving at Shelby at 6.50 p. m.

THE CHARLESTON, CINCINNATI & CHICAGO R. R.

This is a new road, unheard of five years ago. It is one of the best built roads in the South. Every one, upon seeing this road, is instantly impressed with the beauty and durability of the track; the steel rail used weighs 65 lbs. This line now has 150 miles in operation from Rutherfordton, N. C., to Camden, S. C. At Camden they make close connection with the South Carolina railway for Charleston, Columbia, etc. They use coal-burning engines of the best make, and the coaches are all new and first-class. Mail and passenger trains run every day. Leave Shelby at 10.50 A. M., arriving at Charleston at 9.20 P. M.; leave Charleston at 7 A. M., arriving at Shelby at 5.40 P. M. Close connection is made also at Blackburg, S. C., with the Richmond and Danville trains North and South.

E. M. BEAM

has been in business in Shelby about 15 years. Mr. Beam attends closely to his business, has made money, and owns a great deal of real estate. He handles quantities of groceries and lime.

J. J. M'MURRY

was born and raised in Cleveland county. He owns town and country property and conducts one of the largest dry goods houses in Shelby. The size of his store-room is 26 by 110 feet. Mr. McMurry does a very large general merchandise business.

M. L. PUTNAM

has been a resident of Shelby for 33 years, and is an experienced workman and always gives satisfaction. He carries a nice line of watches, clocks and jewelry.

S. G. BRICE

is one of the most substantial and successful business men of Shelby. He at present represents one of the finest wards of the town in the Board of Aldermen. He is a native of South Carolina, but has made his home in Shelby for the past ten years. His handsome residence at once attracts the attention of visitors to the town. Mr. Brice handles large quantities of commercial fertilizers, and is one of our largest cotton buyers. He has met with much success in the mercantile line, and has branch stores at Waco and Bostic stations on the C. C. Railroad.

D. M. BAKER

opened his hardware store here but a few years ago. At that time the most sanguine scarcely dared to think that a strictly hardware store could succeed in Shelby, but Mr. Baker has made a grand success of it, and now has a large wholesale as well as retail trade.

C. E. FRICK,

a native of Baltimore, Md., is one of the ediiors of "The New Era" newspaper. He has established a land ageney, and has many tracts of valuable land for sale. Any one wishing to purchase real estate of any kind will do well to call on him.

MISS SUE PALMER

is successor to Miss Pattie Ramsey in the millinery business. She carries a large line of all the latest styles of millinery goods, and she has a large and increasing trade. This well established house needs no recommendation to the people of Shelby and the surrounding country.

DR. J. C. GIDNEY'S

Pharmacy, on Warren street, is equipped with all the requirements of a first-class drug store. He bought a new soda fountain last year at a cost of $1,300. Dr. Gidney has been a practitioner in Shelby since 1886. He is a graduate of Jefferson Medical College, of Philadelphia. The Doctor is very popular, enjoys a good practice, and carries a large assortment of drugs and medicines.

J. F. HARRIS

is one of the oldest merchants in Shelby. He carries a nice line of family groceries, fresh candies and many other useful articles. He manufactures and repairs tin ware and sells tin plate. Mr. Harris needs no recommendation in Shelby for nice goods and polite attention.

D. AUGUSTUS BEAM

sells an immense number of wagons, buggies, road carts, cane mills and evaporators. He also carries a line of staple groceries. Mr. Beam is a progressive young man and owns a great deal of town and country property.

J. H. HIGHTOWER

manufactures and repairs all kinds of tin and copper,—makes a specialty of tin roofing and guttering,—manufactures evaporators, and has had a large demand for the same since our people began the culture of sorghum cane. He also carries a stock of manufactured tin and tin plate. Mr. Hightower is an experienced workman and does good work.

ALBERT GREEN

is agent for several good fire and life insurance companies. Any one desiring insurance will do well to call on him.

J. T. GARDNER

has just opened a stock of fresh drugs and medicines. Mr. Gardner has had a great deal of experience in the drug business. He is of the late firm of Gardner & Quinn, who were burned out last fall. Mr. Gardner has reopened at the same old stand, and now has a first-class drug store, complete in all its departments.

MRS. LOULA KENDRICK

has recently opened a fashionable millinery establishment, where can be found all the latest styles of everything usually kept in a first-class millinery house.

F. V. HENDRICK

is the successor of the late firm of Wilson & Hendrick. Mr. Hendrick carries a nice stock of dry goods, and has a good and constantly increasing trade.

WRAY & SUTTLE,

one of the old land-marks of Shelby, have as well equipped livery outfits as are to be found in towns much larger than Shelby. The members of the firm are good judges of horses, and select with care all the stock they purchase. They can furnish a turnout to suit the demands of all classes.

THE SHELBY HOTEL,

of long established popularity, having been recently refitted and occupied by J. W. Kerr, the present proprietor, is considered to be one of the best kept hotels in Western North Carolina. Mr. Kerr is an old hotelist, having been in that business a great part of his life.

W. E. McARTHUR,

the only photographer in Shelby, has been in the business about ten years. Mr. McArthur is a good photographer, and takes pictures by the instantaneous process. His gallery is full of pictures of mountain and railroad scenes.

H. D. LEE & CO.

do a general banking and brokerage business. This company is composed of Maj. H. D. Lee, B. Blanton and S. J. Green, all men of considerable property, and considered as safe as any bank in the State. This bank has been a great convenience to Shelby and the surrounding country.

W. W. McFARLAND

opened a general merchandise business in April, 1888. Mr. McFarland has considerable experience in the merchandise business, is a popular salesman, carries a nice line of dry goods, and is making a grand success of his business.

T. W. EBELTOFT

carries a nice line of books, stationery, &c., &c. Mr. Ebeltoft is a great favorite with the people of Shelby. He makes a specialty of school books, and any one desiring anything in his line will find his prices moderate.

W. P. LOVE & CO.

have been in the furniture business in Shelby for a number of years. Their establishment would be an acquisition to any town. They carry a large and well selected stock of all kinds of furniture, and everything usually kept in a first-class furniture establishment is here found.

C. P. ROBERTS, JOB PRINTER.

The subject of this notice is a man out of a thousand who would battle for prosperity against monster repetitions of that life and property destroyer—fire. Twice burned out, the first time with nothing left save the good reputation and extensive trade established by frugal economy and hard work,—the last time by a reasonable amount of insurance sufficient to partly restock his materials,—notwithstanding all these odds against him he to-day is almost without a parallel. Mr. Roberts is a young man but an old printer, having been constantly engaged in the business for the space of fifteen years. Being quick to perceive and quicker to act, he has acquainted himself with all the new ideas of this age in the art of printing, and this, more than all else, accounts for his reaching so far into the hearts and pockets of a generous public. With a new outfit, and with increased advantages such as he has not enjoyed before, he continues to cater to the wants of his patrons. His office is now in the Damron brick block, up stairs, at which place in future as in the past, he aims at making both his work and prices maintain for him the good name heretofore won.

S. L. GILLESPIE

is agent for Ludden & Bates' Southern Music House. Mr. Gillespie established this agency in September, 1884, and has met with splendid success, which shows that the people of Cleveland county take an interest in music as well as money making. Mr. Gillespie carries a full line of musical merchandise. Any one in need of such will do well to call on him.

JNO. F. HARRIS,

GROCER AND CONFECTIONER,

ALSO MANUFACTURER OF
And Dealer in

ALL KINDS OF TIN-WARE,

LaFayette st., *Shelby, N. C.*

THE CITY MARKET,

LaFayette and Marion sts., *Shelby, N. C.*

MALLARD & LEAK, Proprietors.

DAILY SUPPLY OF THE BEST MEATS TO BE FOUND.

☞ Orders from other towns solicited.

V. McBrayer, M. D. H. D. Wilson.

McBRAYER & WILSON

HAVE THE

LARGEST DRUG EMPORIUM IN

Western North Carolina.

They keep first-class Drugs, Medicines, Chemicals, Fancy and Toilet Articles, Jewelry, Etc., Etc.

LaFayette st., SHELBY, N. C.

☞ Physicians prescriptions carefully compounded.

Julius A. Wray,

LaFayette street, *SHELBY, N. C.*

LIVERY, FEED

—AND—

SALE STABLES.

BEST VEHICLES,

Good Gentle Horses,

POLITE AND ATTENTIVE DRIVERS.

Prices Moderate.

☞ Hacks meet all trains, and convey passengers to Cleveland Springs.

Dr. J. C. GIDNEY,

Corner Warren and LaFayette streets,

SHELBY, N. C.,

DEALER IN

Drugs,
Medicines,
Chemicals,
Paints and Oils,
Garden, Grass
and Clover Seed.

Fancy and
Toilet Articles,
Trusses,
Lamps,
Brushes,
Perfumery,

CIGARS, TOBACCO, &c., &c.

Physicians' prescriptions carefully compounded, and orders answered with care and despatch. Our stock of Medicine is complete, warranted genuine, and of the best quality.

T. W. EBELTOFT,

DEALER IN

Books,

Stationery,

Art Material,

Rubber Stamps, Etc.,

SHELBY, N. C.

J. A. Anthony,

Attorney at Law,

SHELBY, N. C.

☞ Office in Miller Bros. Block, 1st east room, up stairs.

D. M. BAKER,

Wholesale and retail dealer in

HARDWARE GUNS, CUTLERY.

AGRICULTURAL IMPLEMENTS, ETC., ETC.

Marion street, Shelby, N. C.

Dr. L. N. DURHAM,

SURGEON DENTIST,

Beam Building,

LaFayette street,

SHELBY, N. C.

Albert Green,

SHELBY, N. C.,

LIFE AND FIRE

Insurance Agent.

B. F. WOOD. J. F. SCHENCK.

WOOD & SCHENCK,

Attorneys at Law,

SHELBY, N. C.

J. W. GIDNEY. J. L. WEBB.

GIDNEY & WEBB,

Attorneys at Law,

SHELBY, N. C.

Practice in the State and Federal courts.
Collections promptly made.

S. L. TOMLINSON,

An Artistic Barber

AND FASHIONABLE HAIR DRESSER,

SHELBY, N. C.

Having located in Shelby, I respectfully solicit the patronage of the town and surrounding country.

Shaving done as good as the best.

Hair cut in the latest style.

All work guaranteed to please.

Shop in the rear of W. P. Love's furniture store.

G. W. WRAY. C. B. SUTTLE.

SHELBY

LIVERY STABLES.

LIVERY, FEED AND SALE.

BEST

HORSES

AND VEHICLES

Always on Hand.

All kinds of Conveyances always ready to Convey persons to any point in Western North and South Carolina, with polite and attentive drivers, and all at moderate prices.

WRAY & SUTTLE,

Proprietors.

Marion street, Shelby, N. C.

IN CONCLUSION,

It is well to here state that about May 1st this pamphlet was nearly all printed and would soon been ready for distribution, but Messrs. C. P. Robe Co. (by whom the work was being done) fell a vict the late fire in Shelby, when most everything und roof was a total destruction. This has caused an reproduction of the book, subjecting the publis much loss, inconvenience and delay in making it for distribution. Several of the finest cuts do not a which would have graced its pages, notably—those residence of Capt. Bell, the Central Hotel, the Cleveland Springs, and others, which the publish not had time to replace.

In speaking of the various business houses and prises of Shelby, all are not mentioned, as they a advertisers in this book. But Shelby invites all to and help utilize and partake of our advantages, a as to enjoy our invigorating climate. PUBLISH

www.ingramcontent.com/pod-product-compliance
Lightning Source LLC
Chambersburg PA
CBHW022025080426
42733CB00007B/737
* 9 7 8 3 3 3 7 2 5 4 3 8 4 *